GW00374666

FILM & TV JOURNAL

THIS JOURNAL BELONGS TO:

....

STARTED: ....

FINISHED: ....

TOP 10
FILMS &
TV SHOWS

1 ....

2 ....

3 ....

4 ....

5 ....

6 ....

7 ....

8 ....

9 ....

10 ....

FILM/SHOW

DATE WATCHED

RATING

REVIEW

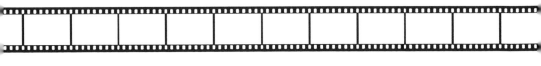

NOTES

FILM/SHOW	DATE WATCHED	RATING

RATING ☆☆☆☆☆

REVIEW

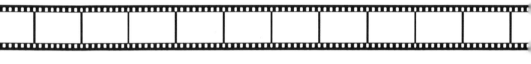

NOTES

FILM/SHOW	DATE WATCHED	RATING
		☆☆☆☆☆

REVIEW

NOTES

| FILM/SHOW | DATE WATCHED | RATING |

RATING ☆☆☆☆☆

REVIEW

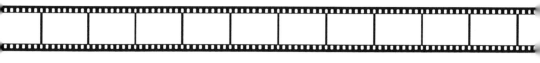

NOTES

| FILM/SHOW | DATE WATCHED | RATING |

REVIEW

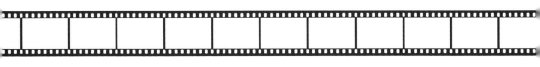

NOTES

FILM/SHOW	DATE WATCHED	RATING ☆☆☆☆☆

REVIEW

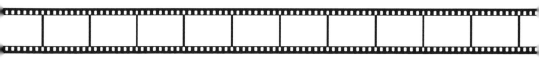

NOTES

FILM/SHOW	DATE WATCHED	RATING ☆☆☆☆☆

REVIEW

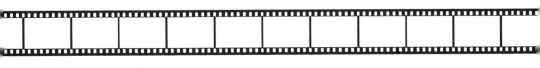

NOTES

FILM/SHOW	DATE WATCHED	RATING
		☆☆☆☆☆

REVIEW

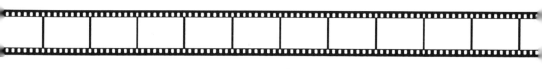

NOTES

FILM/SHOW	DATE WATCHED	RATING
		☆☆☆☆☆

REVIEW

NOTES

FILM/SHOW	DATE WATCHED	RATING
		☆☆☆☆☆

REVIEW

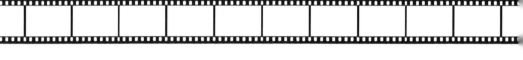

NOTES

| FILM/SHOW | DATE WATCHED | RATING ☆☆☆☆☆ |

REVIEW

NOTES

| FILM/SHOW | DATE WATCHED | RATING ☆☆☆☆☆ |

REVIEW

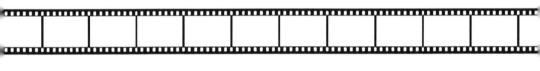

NOTES

FILM/SHOW	DATE WATCHED	RATING
		☆ ☆ ☆ ☆ ☆

REVIEW

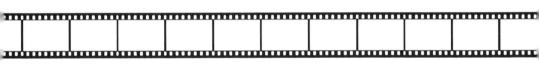

NOTES

FILM/SHOW

DATE WATCHED

RATING

REVIEW

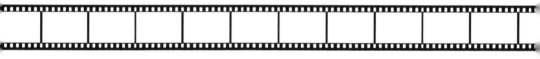

NOTES

FILM/SHOW	DATE WATCHED	RATING
		☆☆☆☆☆

REVIEW

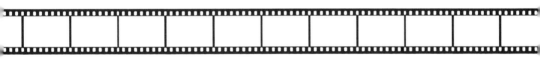

NOTES

FILM/SHOW	DATE WATCHED	RATING

REVIEW

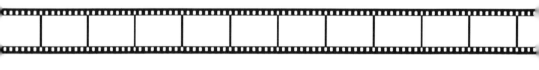

NOTES

FILM/SHOW

DATE WATCHED

RATING
☆ ☆ ☆ ☆ ☆

REVIEW

NOTES

| FILM/SHOW | DATE WATCHED | RATING ☆☆☆☆☆ |

REVIEW

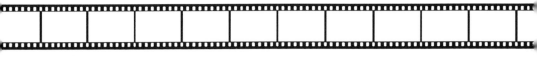

NOTES

FILM/SHOW	DATE WATCHED	RATING ☆☆☆☆☆

REVIEW

NOTES

| FILM/SHOW | DATE WATCHED | RATING ☆☆☆☆☆ |

REVIEW

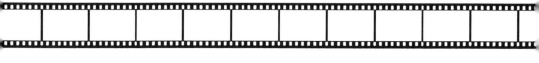

NOTES

FILM/SHOW	DATE WATCHED	RATING
		☆☆☆☆☆

REVIEW

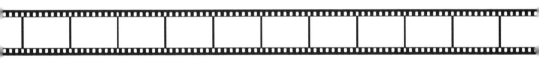

NOTES

| FILM/SHOW | DATE WATCHED | RATING |

REVIEW

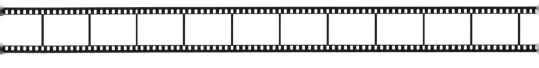

NOTES

FILM/SHOW	DATE WATCHED	RATING
		☆ ☆ ☆ ☆ ☆

REVIEW

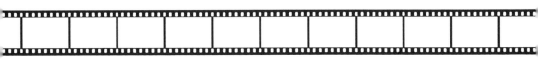

NOTES

FILM/SHOW DATE WATCHED RATING
☆ ☆ ☆ ☆ ☆

REVIEW

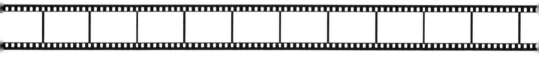

NOTES

FILM/SHOW	DATE WATCHED	RATING
		☆☆☆☆☆

REVIEW

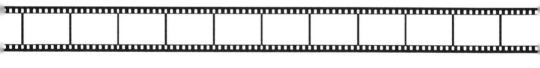

NOTES

FILM/SHOW	DATE WATCHED	RATING
		☆☆☆☆☆

REVIEW

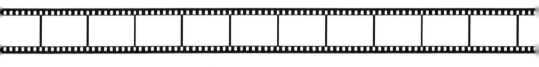

NOTES

FILM/SHOW	DATE WATCHED	RATING

REVIEW

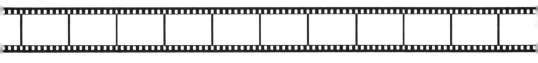

NOTES

FILM/SHOW	DATE WATCHED	RATING
		☆☆☆☆☆

REVIEW

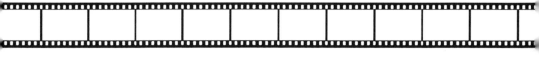

NOTES

FILM/SHOW	DATE WATCHED	RATING
		☆☆☆☆☆

REVIEW

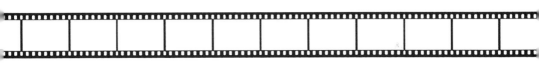

NOTES

| FILM/SHOW | DATE WATCHED | RATING |

REVIEW

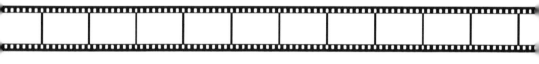

NOTES

| FILM/SHOW | DATE WATCHED | RATING |

REVIEW

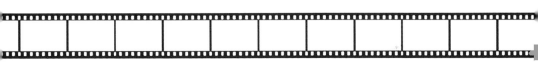

NOTES

FILM/SHOW	DATE WATCHED	RATING
		☆ ☆ ☆ ☆ ☆

REVIEW

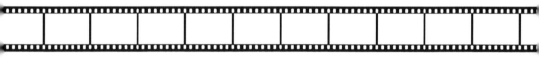

NOTES

FILM/SHOW	DATE WATCHED	RATING

REVIEW

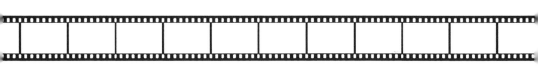

NOTES

FILM/SHOW   DATE WATCHED   RATING
☆☆☆☆☆

REVIEW

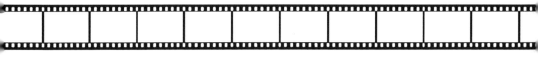

NOTES

REVIEW

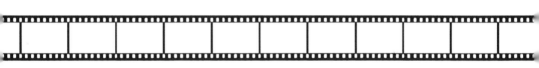

NOTES

FILM/SHOW	DATE WATCHED	RATING
		☆☆☆☆☆

REVIEW

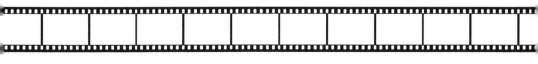

NOTES

FILM/SHOW	DATE WATCHED	RATING
		☆☆☆☆☆

REVIEW

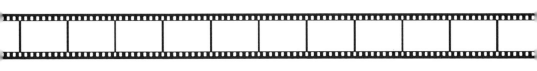

NOTES

| FILM/SHOW | DATE WATCHED | RATING ☆☆☆☆☆ |

REVIEW

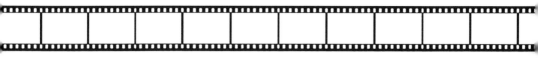

NOTES

FILM/SHOW	DATE WATCHED	RATING

REVIEW

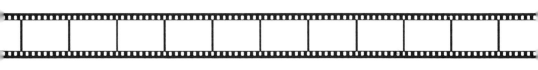

NOTES

| FILM/SHOW | DATE WATCHED | RATING ☆☆☆☆☆ |

REVIEW

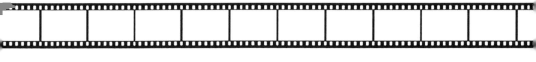

NOTES

FILM/SHOW	DATE WATCHED	RATING
		☆ ☆ ☆ ☆ ☆

REVIEW

NOTES

FILM/SHOW	DATE WATCHED	RATING
		☆ ☆ ☆ ☆ ☆

REVIEW

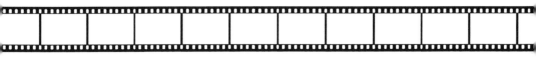

NOTES

FILM/SHOW	DATE WATCHED	RATING
		☆ ☆ ☆ ☆ ☆

REVIEW

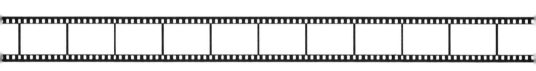

NOTES

| FILM/SHOW | DATE WATCHED | RATING ☆☆☆☆☆ |

REVIEW

NOTES

FILM/SHOW	DATE WATCHED	RATING
		☆ ☆ ☆ ☆ ☆

REVIEW

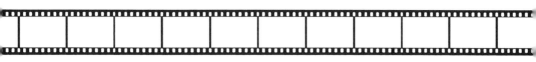

NOTES

| FILM/SHOW | DATE WATCHED | RATING ☆☆☆☆☆ |

REVIEW

NOTES

FILM/SHOW	DATE WATCHED	RATING ☆☆☆☆☆

REVIEW

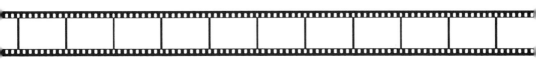

NOTES

| FILM/SHOW | DATE WATCHED | RATING ☆☆☆☆☆ |

REVIEW

NOTES

FILM/SHOW
DATE WATCHED
RATING

REVIEW

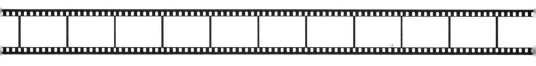

NOTES

| FILM/SHOW | DATE WATCHED | RATING ☆☆☆☆☆ |

REVIEW

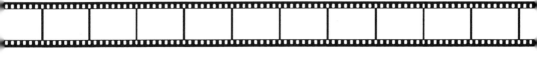

NOTES

FILM/SHOW	DATE WATCHED	RATING

REVIEW

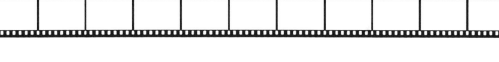

NOTES

FILM/SHOW

DATE WATCHED

RATING

REVIEW

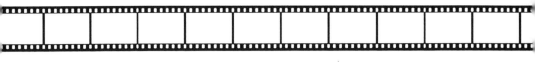

NOTES

FILM/SHOW	DATE WATCHED	RATING
		☆☆☆☆☆

REVIEW

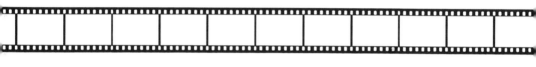

NOTES

| FILM/SHOW | DATE WATCHED | RATING ☆☆☆☆☆ |

REVIEW

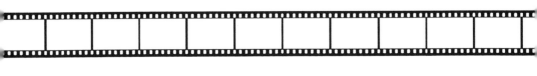

NOTES

FILM/SHOW	DATE WATCHED	RATING ☆☆☆☆☆

REVIEW

NOTES

FILM/SHOW

DATE WATCHED

RATING

☆ ☆ ☆ ☆ ☆

REVIEW

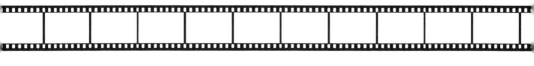

NOTES

FILM/SHOW	DATE WATCHED	RATING

RATING ☆☆☆☆☆

REVIEW

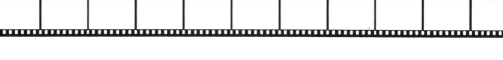

NOTES

FILM/SHOW	DATE WATCHED	RATING
		☆☆☆☆☆

REVIEW

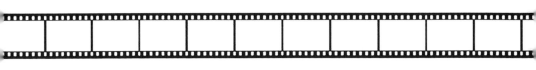

NOTES

| FILM/SHOW | DATE WATCHED | RATING ☆☆☆☆☆ |

REVIEW

NOTES

FILM/SHOW	DATE WATCHED	RATING

REVIEW

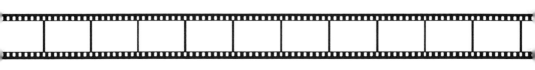

NOTES

| FILM/SHOW | DATE WATCHED | RATING ☆☆☆☆☆ |

REVIEW

NOTES

FILM/SHOW	DATE WATCHED	RATING

REVIEW

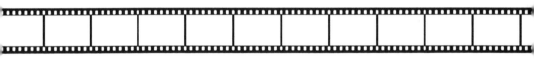

NOTES

FILM/SHOW	DATE WATCHED	RATING
		☆☆☆☆☆

REVIEW

NOTES

| FILM/SHOW | DATE WATCHED | RATING ☆☆☆☆☆ |

REVIEW

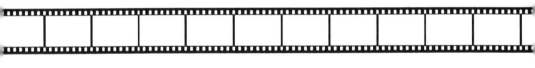

NOTES

FILM/SHOW	DATE WATCHED	RATING
		☆☆☆☆☆

REVIEW

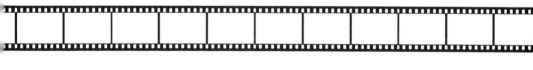

NOTES

| FILM/SHOW | DATE WATCHED | RATING ☆☆☆☆☆ |

REVIEW

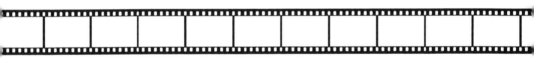

NOTES

FILM/SHOW	DATE WATCHED	RATING
		☆☆☆☆☆

REVIEW

NOTES

FILM/SHOW

DATE WATCHED

RATING
☆ ☆ ☆ ☆ ☆

REVIEW

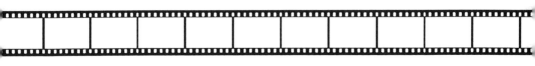

NOTES

FILM/SHOW	DATE WATCHED	RATING
		☆☆☆☆☆

REVIEW

NOTES

| FILM/SHOW | DATE WATCHED | RATING ☆☆☆☆☆ |

REVIEW

NOTES

FILM/SHOW	DATE WATCHED	RATING
		☆☆☆☆☆

REVIEW

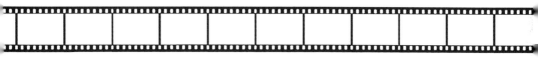

NOTES

FILM/SHOW | DATE WATCHED | RATING

REVIEW

NOTES

| FILM/SHOW | DATE WATCHED | RATING |

REVIEW

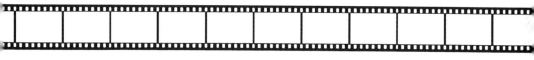

NOTES

FILM/SHOW	DATE WATCHED	RATING
		☆☆☆☆☆

REVIEW

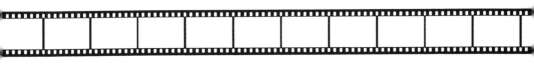

NOTES

FILM/SHOW	DATE WATCHED	RATING ☆☆☆☆☆

REVIEW

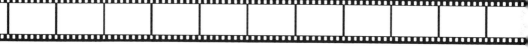

NOTES

| FILM/SHOW | DATE WATCHED | RATING ☆☆☆☆☆ |

REVIEW

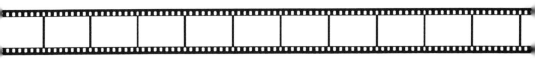

NOTES

FILM/SHOW	DATE WATCHED	RATING
		☆☆☆☆☆

REVIEW

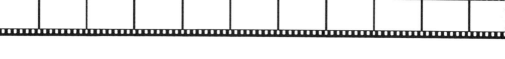

NOTES

| FILM/SHOW | DATE WATCHED | RATING ☆☆☆☆☆ |

REVIEW

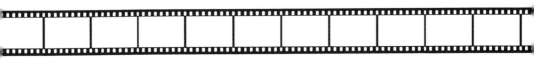

NOTES

REVIEW

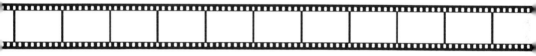

NOTES

FILM/SHOW	DATE WATCHED	RATING

☆ ☆ ☆ ☆ ☆

REVIEW

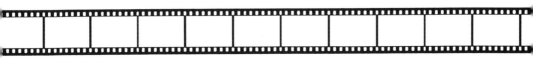

NOTES

FILM/SHOW	DATE WATCHED	RATING
		☆☆☆☆☆

REVIEW

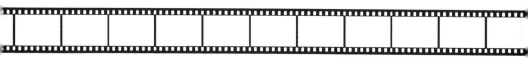

NOTES

| FILM/SHOW | DATE WATCHED | RATING |

REVIEW

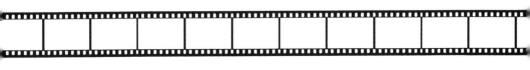

NOTES

| FILM/SHOW | DATE WATCHED | RATING |

☆ ☆ ☆ ☆ ☆

REVIEW

NOTES

| FILM/SHOW | DATE WATCHED | RATING ☆☆☆☆☆ |

REVIEW

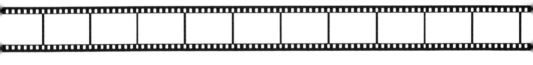

NOTES

FILM/SHOW	DATE WATCHED	RATING

REVIEW

NOTES

FILM/SHOW   DATE WATCHED   RATING

REVIEW

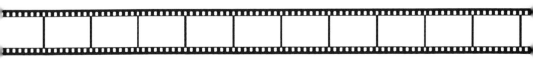

NOTES

FILM/SHOW	DATE WATCHED	RATING
		☆☆☆☆☆

REVIEW

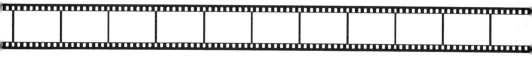

NOTES

FILM/SHOW	DATE WATCHED	RATING
		☆ ☆ ☆ ☆ ☆

REVIEW

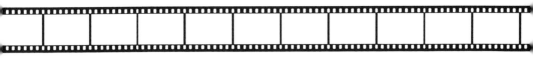

NOTES

FILM/SHOW	DATE WATCHED	RATING
		☆ ☆ ☆ ☆ ☆

REVIEW

NOTES

| FILM/SHOW | DATE WATCHED | RATING |

☆ ☆ ☆ ☆ ☆

REVIEW

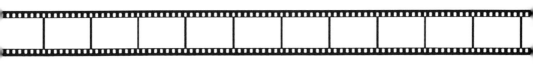

NOTES

| FILM/SHOW | DATE WATCHED | RATING ☆☆☆☆☆ |

REVIEW

NOTES

FILM/SHOW	DATE WATCHED	RATING
		☆☆☆☆☆

REVIEW

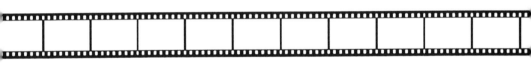

NOTES

FILM/SHOW	DATE WATCHED	RATING ☆☆☆☆☆

REVIEW

NOTES

| FILM/SHOW | DATE WATCHED | RATING |

REVIEW

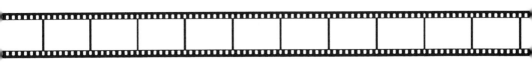

NOTES

FILM/SHOW	DATE WATCHED	RATING

REVIEW

NOTES

FILM/SHOW	DATE WATCHED	RATING
		☆☆☆☆☆

REVIEW

NOTES

FILM/SHOW	DATE WATCHED	RATING
		☆☆☆☆☆

REVIEW

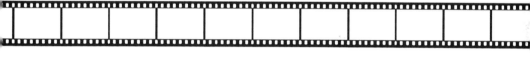

NOTES

FILM/SHOW	DATE WATCHED	RATING
		☆ ☆ ☆ ☆ ☆

REVIEW

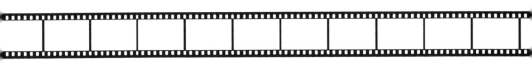

NOTES

Printed in Great Britain
by Amazon

83998422R00059